THE NATURE KIDS GUIDE TO

TURKEYS

DAVID ANDERSON

LP Media Inc. Publishing
Text copyright © 2026 by LP Media Inc.
All rights reserved.

For information address LP Media Inc. Publishing,
30012 Variolite St NW, Princeton MN 55371
www.lpmedia.org

Publication Data

Turkeys
The Nature Kid's Guide to Turkeys — First edition.

Summary: "Learn all about Turkeys, the Nature Kid Way"
— Provided by publisher.

ISBN: 979-8-89818-104-8

[1. Turkeys – Non-Fiction] I. Title.

Title: The Nature Kid's Guide to Turkeys

CONTENTS

FOREST FRIENDS

DID YOU KNOW?

Wild turkeys almost disappeared in the early 1900s. Only about 30,000 were left. People worked hard to bring them back. Now millions live in all 50 states.

Gobble! A wild turkey walks through the trees. It looks for food.

Wild turkeys live in forests across North America. They make their homes where trees grow tall. Oak and pine forests are favorite spots.

But turkeys need open areas too. They search for food in meadows and fields. Forest edges work well because they offer both.

These birds **roost** in trees at night. They fly up to branches when the sun sets. This keeps them safe while they sleep.

Turkeys also like places with water nearby. Streams and ponds help keep them healthy. Good Turkey habitat has food, trees, and water all together.

TURKEY TURF

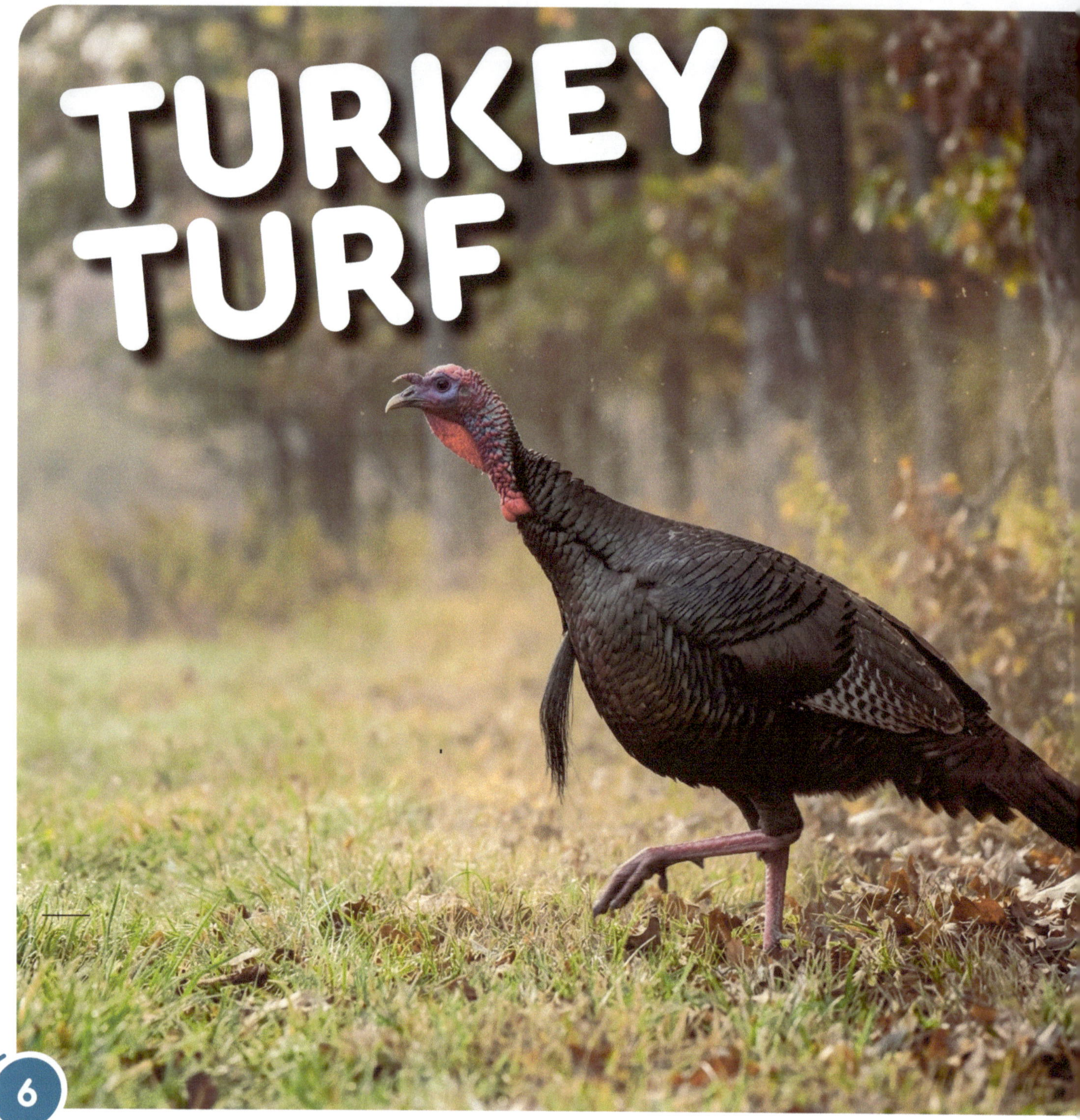

Rustle! A turkey steps through dry leaves and crosses a wide field.

Wild turkeys live in many parts of the United States. They also live in Mexico and Canada.

These birds can survive in different climates. Hot summers and cold winters do not stop them. This helps them adapt to many places.

Turkeys can travel across large areas. A flock may cover several miles in one day. They move to find food, water, and escape predators.

Turkeys can run up to 25 miles per hour. That is faster than most people can sprint.

BIG BIRDS

Stomp! A big turkey struts across the ground. It puffs up its feathers.

Wild turkeys are large birds. They are one of the biggest birds in North America.

Males are especially big. They can weigh up to 24 pounds. Females weigh about half that size. Both have round, heavy bodies.

Turkeys stand tall on long legs. From head to tail, males can reach four feet long. This big size helps them stay warm in winter.

Male turkeys have a fleshy flap called a snood. It changes color when excited.

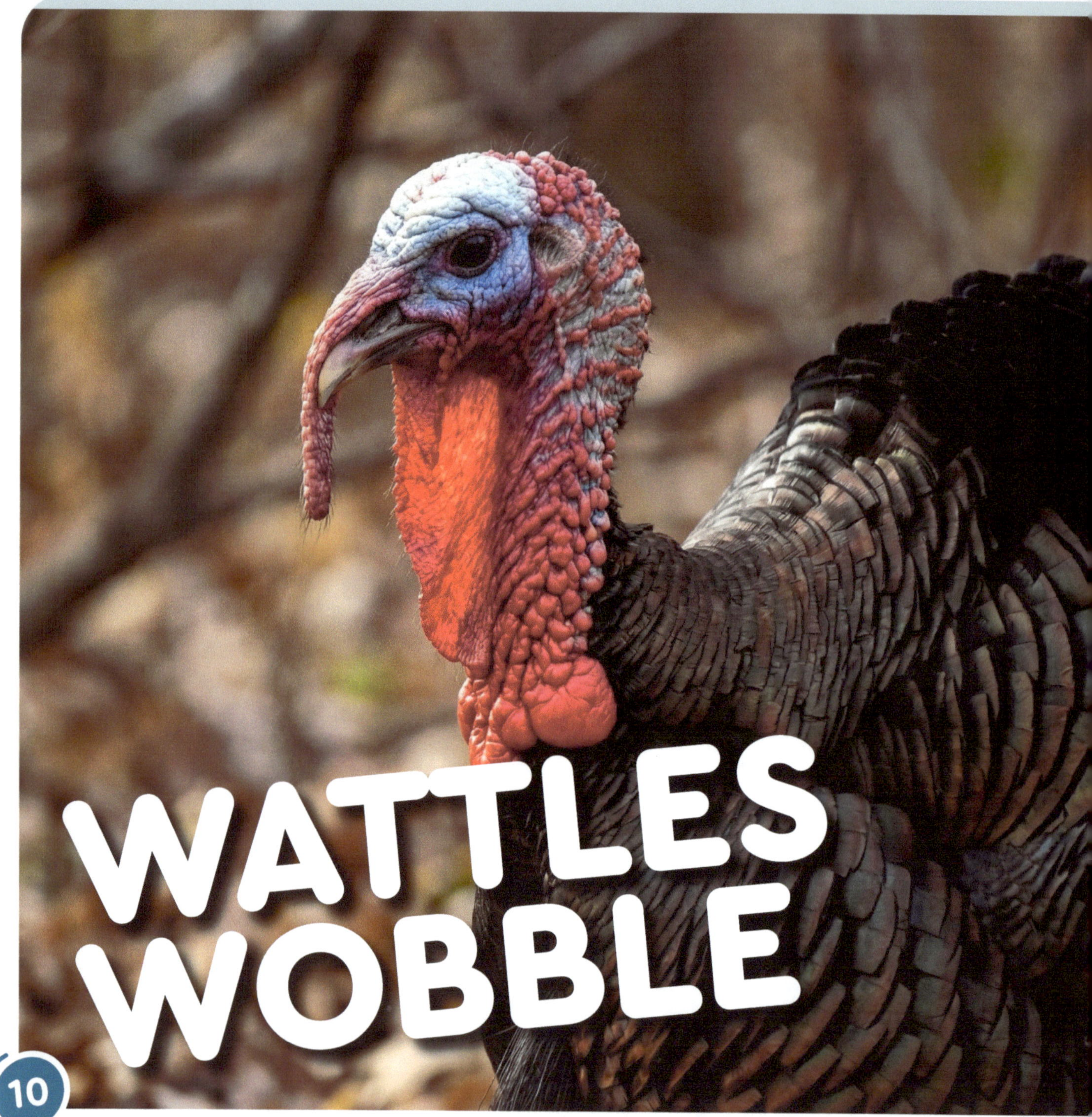

10

Droop! A red flap of skin hangs from a turkey's neck.

The red skin under a turkey's chin is called a **wattle**. It hangs down and wobbles when the bird moves. Both males and females have wattles, but males have bigger ones.

The wattle can also change color. It turns bright red when a male is excited.

Turkeys have a **snood** too. This is the fleshy bump above the beak. It can stretch and hang down over the beak. The snood also changes color from red to blue.

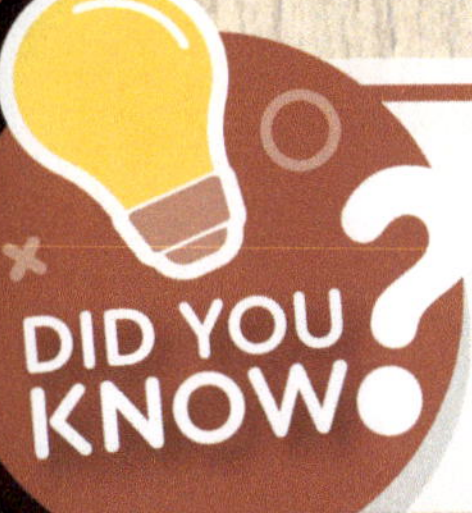

DID YOU KNOW? A turkey's wattle and snood help control body temperature in hot weather.

11

SHARP
SENSES

Snap! A turkey turns its head. It hears a tiny sound.

Turkeys have amazing eyesight. With eyes on the sides of their head, they can see almost all around their body, without even turning their neck!

They spot movement from far away. This helps them see danger coming.

Turkeys hear very well too. They can hear sounds from a mile away. Sharp senses keep them safe.

Turkeys see 3 times better than humans with 270-degree vision!

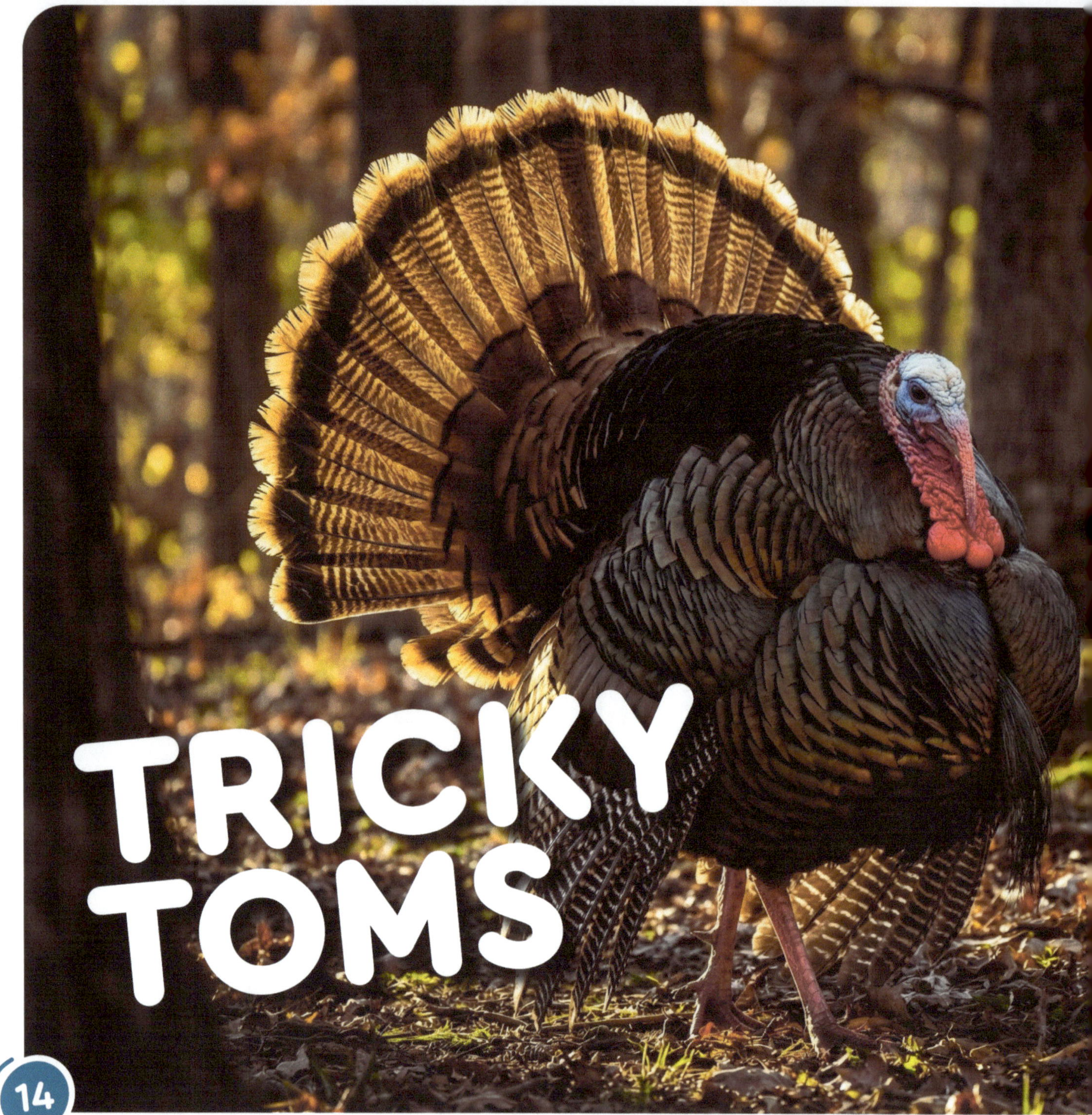

14

Squawk! A turkey spreads its tail wide. This makes it look huge.

Turkeys have smart ways to stay safe. When a predator comes close, turkeys puff up their feathers. This makes them look much bigger than they really are.

Male turkeys fan out their tail feathers. This wide display can scare off some enemies.

Turkeys also use their sharp spurs to fight back. These bony points grow on their legs. A kick can hurt a predator badly.

Turkeys can fly short distances at speeds up to 55 miles per hour to escape danger.

16

Crunch! A turkey pecks at seeds on the ground. It searches for a tasty meal.

Turkeys eat many different foods. They munch on acorns, nuts, and berries. Seeds and grains are favorites too.

These birds also eat bugs. Grasshoppers, beetles, and snails make tasty snacks. Young turkeys eat lots of insects to grow strong.

Turkeys swallow small stones called grit. The stones help grind up food in their stomachs. This helps them digest tough nuts and seeds.

Turkeys can eat up to 200 ticks in just one single day. Talk about helpful birds!

SCRATCH SEARCH

Scratch! A turkey drags its feet through dirt and leaves.

Turkeys use their feet to find food. They scratch the ground with their strong claws. This uncovers hidden treats beneath leaves and soil.

They kick backward with one foot, then the other. This clears away dirt and debris so they can peck at what they find underneath.

Turkeys scratch in forests and fields. They search for buried acorns, roots, and worms. Tasty grubs hide in the soil too.

A turkey may scratch the same spot many times. This helps them find every hidden treat.

WATCH OUT!

A Coyote stands silently in tall grass. He's waiting for his chance.

Many animals hunt turkeys. Hawks and owls attack from above. They swoop down to catch young turkeys by surprise.

Coyotes and foxes chase turkeys on the ground. These hunters are fast and sneaky. They hide and wait for the right moment.

Bobcats also hunt turkeys. They creep through the forest quietly. Even turkey nests are not safe. Raccoons and snakes eat turkey eggs and baby chicks.

Great horned owls can hunt turkeys at night when they roost in trees.

21

RUN AND HIDE

Whoosh! A turkey dashes into thick bushes to hide.

Turkeys have ways to stay safe. Running is their first choice. They can sprint away from danger quickly.

Hiding works well too. Turkeys crouch low in tall grass. Their brown feathers blend in with the forest floor.

At night, turkeys fly up into trees. They roost on high branches where predators cannot reach them.

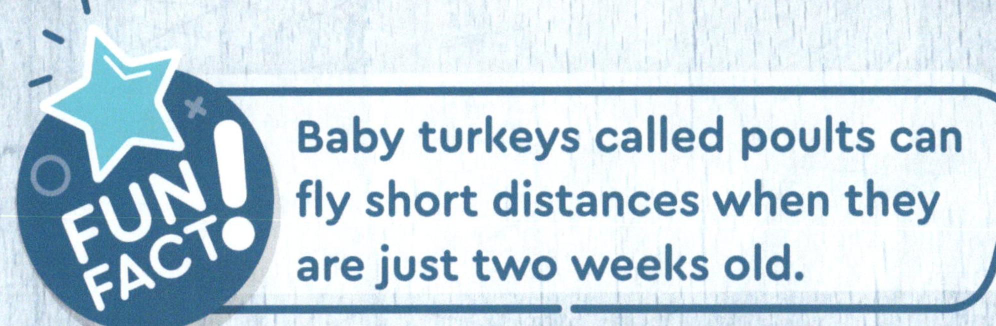

FAST FEET

Thump! A turkey runs across a meadow on strong legs.

Turkeys are fast runners. Their long legs help them move quickly. They can reach speeds up to 25 miles per hour.

Turkeys walk a lot each day. They travel through forests and fields.

Turkeys can also fly short distances. They flap hard to reach tree branches. But turkeys usually run to escape danger. They only fly when they must.

Turkey legs have scales like their dinosaur ancestors. Their feet have four toes with claws.

DAY LIFE

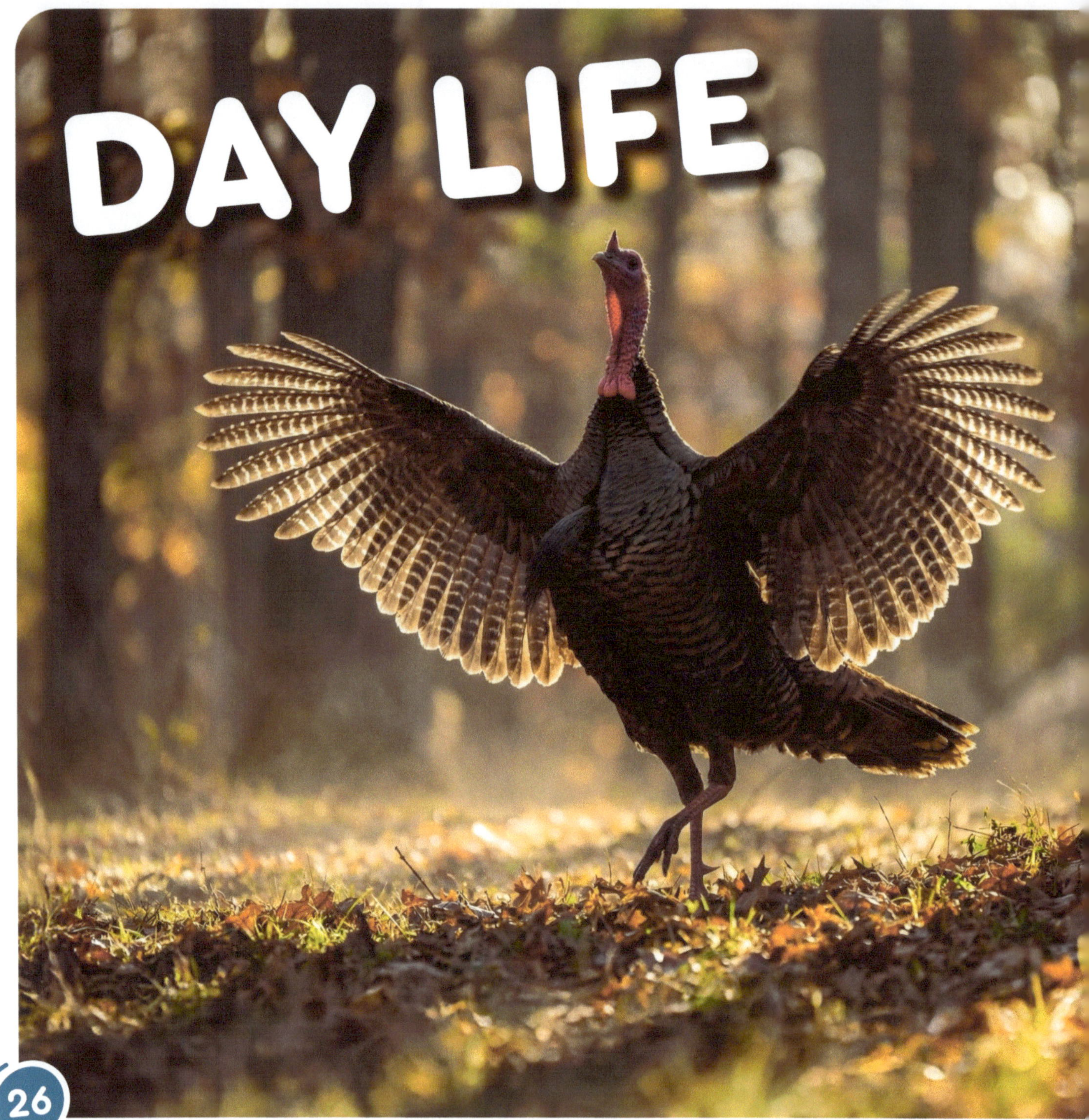

Chirp! The sun rises over the trees. A turkey wakes up and stretches.

Turkeys are busy during the day. They wake up at dawn and fly down from their sleeping trees.

Mornings are for eating. Turkeys walk slowly and peck at the ground.

In the afternoon, turkeys rest in shady spots. They also clean their feathers. This is called preening.

Before sunset, turkeys fly up to high branches to sleep.

Turkeys remember where they found food. They return to the same spots day after day to eat.

FLOCK TOGETHER
28

Cluck! Several turkeys walk together through a sunny clearing.

Turkeys live in groups called flocks. A flock can have as few as five and as many as fifty birds.

Hens often stay together with their young. They help each other watch for danger. Many eyes spot predators faster than just two.

Male turkeys form their own groups. Young males are called Jakes. They travel in small bands together. Older males called Toms may join them too.

Turkeys make more than 20 different sounds to communicate with their flock members!

STRUT STUFF

Puff! A male turkey fans out his tail feathers wide.

Tom turkeys put on a big show. They puff up their bodies and spread their tails. This makes their feathers shine in the sunlight.

Toms also make a loud gobbling sound. This noise can travel far and tells other turkeys they are nearby.

Toms drag their wings on the ground too. This makes a drumming sound. Their heads turn bright red and blue.

A male turkey's gobble can be heard up to one mile away. Only males gobble. Females make a clicking sound instead.

TINY POULTS

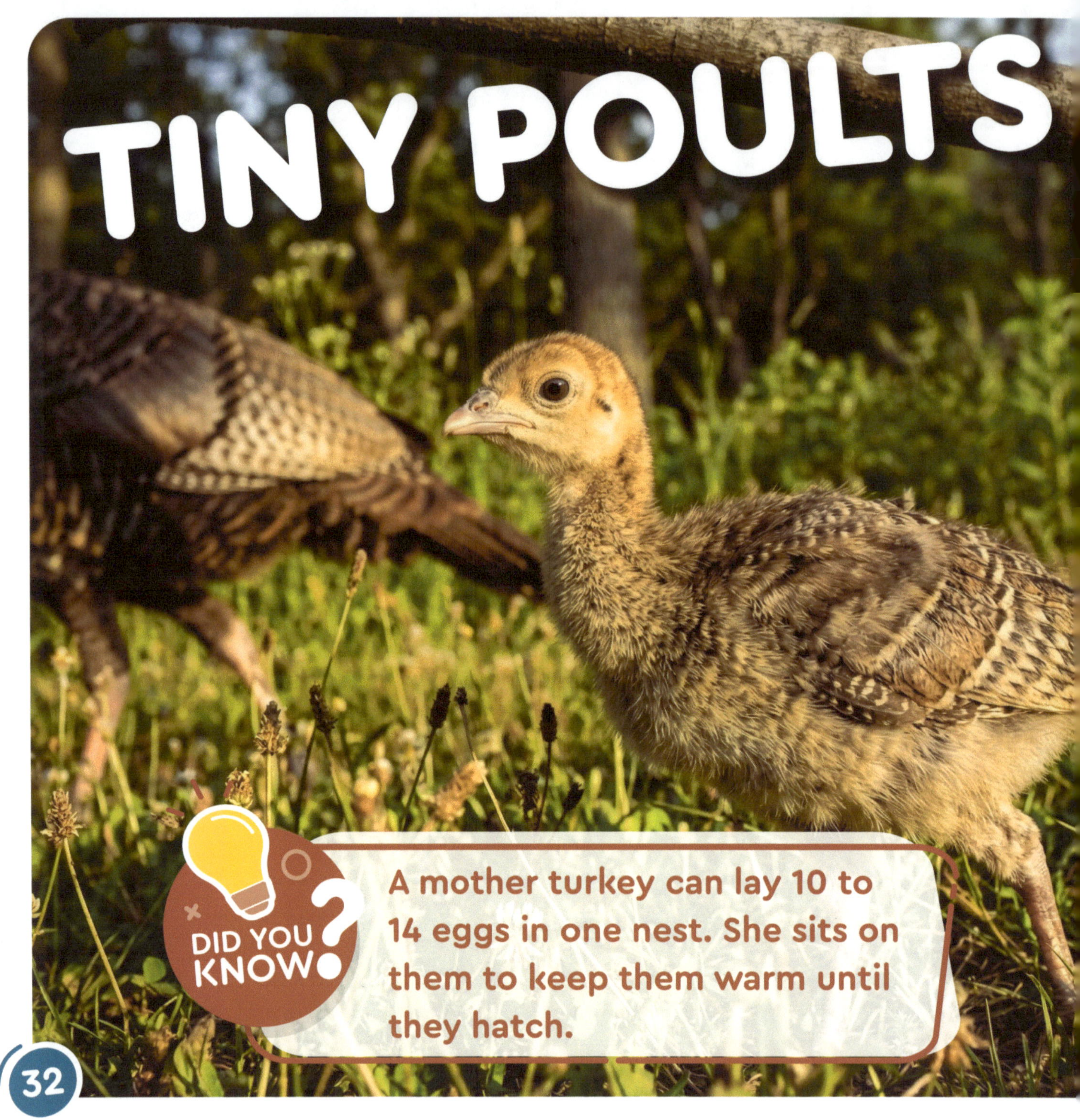

DID YOU KNOW?
A mother turkey can lay 10 to 14 eggs in one nest. She sits on them to keep them warm until they hatch.

Peep! A fuzzy baby turkey follows its mother through tall grass.

Baby turkeys are called **poults**. They hatch from eggs after about 28 days. Poults can walk and find food right away.

Poults are covered in soft, fluffy down that is tan and brown. This coloring helps them hide in grass and leaves.

Poults grow fast. They can fly short distances when they are two weeks old. By fall, young turkeys look almost like adults.

Poults stay close to their mother. She keeps them warm and safe from danger.

STICK CLOSE

Grunt! A mother turkey leads her poults to safety.

Mother turkeys raise their young alone. They keep poults safe, but the young turkeys feed themselves.

Hens build nests on the ground. They pick hidden spots. A nest may hold ten to twelve eggs.

Mothers sit on eggs for almost a month. Their brown feathers blend in with the forest floor.

Hens teach poults what to eat. They show them how to find bugs and seeds. Mothers also warn poults when danger is near.

DID YOU KNOW?

A hen may walk her poults up to one mile each day looking for food.

TALENTED TURKEYS

Gobble, gobble! A turkey puffs up its feathers.

Turkeys have amazing skills. They can fly up to 55 miles per hour in short bursts. They also run fast on the ground.

Turkeys have great eyesight. They can see in color. Their eyes sit on the sides of their heads. This helps them spot danger all around.

Turkeys remember places well. They know where to find food and water.

Turkeys have a magnetic compass in their brains! Some scientists believe this helps them find their way home over long distances.

MAMA KNOWS

Gobble! A mother turkey walks with her chicks.

Hens keep their poults warm under their wings. They also protect them from danger.

Poults learn by watching their mother. She shows them how to find food. She teaches them what is safe to eat.

By four months, they look almost like adults. Young males leave their mother in late fall to join other young males. Females often stay with their mother through the first winter.

FUN FACT!

Turkey poults can walk and follow their mother just one day after they hatch.

GLOSSARY

roost
To sleep on a high branch in a tree.

wattle
The red flap of skin that hangs under a turkey's chin.

snood
The bumpy piece of skin that hangs over a turkey's beak.

grit
Tiny stones that birds swallow to help crush their food.

poults
Baby turkeys that have just hatched from eggs.